D0847210

MIXED MEDIA SKILLS LAB

SANDEE EWASIUK

CRABTREE
PUBLISHING COMPANY
WWW.CRABTREEBOOKS.COM

ART SKILLS LAB

Author
Sandee Ewasiuk

Editors
Marcia Abramson, Reagan Miller

Photo research
Melissa McClellan

Cover/Interior Design
T.J. Choleva

Project Designer
Sandee Ewasiuk

Proofreader
Kathy Middleton

**Production coordinator
and Prepress technician**
Tammy McGarr

Print coordinator
Katherine Berti

Developed and produced for
Crabtree Publishing by
BlueApple*Works* Inc.

Consultant
Trevor Hodgson
Fine artist and former director of The Dundas Valley School of Art

Art & Photographs
Shutterstock.com: © Emena (cover bottom left); © urfin (cover middle right); © Excellent backgrounds (background); © Monkey Business Images (p. 4 left); © Ruslan Kokarev (p. 5 middle right); ©AntoinetteW (p. 5 top left); © Ann Baldwin (p. 5 bottom left); © Lyudmila Suvorova (p.6 top left); © James John Harris (p.6 top middle left); Room's Studio (p.6 top middle right); © Aigars Reinholds (p.6 top right); © Gilmanshin (p. 6 bottom left); © Pj Aun(p.6 bottom middle left); © Be Good (p.6 bottom middle right); © Banana Republic images (p. 6 middle); © hideto999 (p. 6 middle right); © Imageman (p.6 bottom right); © Afonkin_Y (p. 6 bottom); © Lopolo (p. 18 top);

© Austen Photography (cover, title page, TOC, p. 7– 29)

Instructive paintings © Sandee Ewasiuk cover, p. 7– 29 excluding bios
p. 4 Paul Klee/The Berggruen Klee Collection, 1984/Public Domain
p. 5 bottom right © Estate of Carl Beam
p. 9 Edvard Munch/National Gallery of Norway/Public Domain
p. 11 © Julie Mehretu/The Museum of Modem Art/Digital Image © The Museum of Modem Art/Licensed by SCALA /Art Resource, NY
p. 13 KJP1/Creative Commons
p. 15 © Judy Chicago/SOCAN (2018)/ Photo courtesy of Judy Chicago / Art Resource, NY
p. 25 © Estate of Kurt Schwitters / SOCAN (2018) / Philadelphia Museum of Art/ Photo Credit: The Philadelphia Museum of Art / Art Resource, NY
p. 27 © Estate of Thornton Dial / SOCAN (2018) / Photo Credit: American Folk Art Museum / Art Resource, NY
p. 29 Public Domain

Library and Archives Canada Cataloguing in Publication

Ewasiuk, Sandee, author
    Mixed media skills lab / Sandee Ewasiuk.

(Art skills lab)
Includes index.
Issued in print and electronic formats.
ISBN 978-0-7787-5222-6 (hardcover).--
ISBN 978-0-7787-5235-6 (softcover).--
ISBN 978-1-4271-2179-0 (HTML)

    1. Mixed media (Art)--Technique--Juvenile literature.
2. Mixed media (Art)--Juvenile literature.
3. Handicraft--Juvenile literature. I. Title.

TT160.E93 2018   j702.81   C2018-905550-2
                                   C2018-905551-0

Library of Congress Cataloging-in-Publication Data

Names: Ewasiuk, Sandee, author.
Title: Mixed media skills lab / Sandee Ewasiuk.
Description: New York, New York : Crabtree Publishing, [2019] |
  Series: Art skills lab | Includes index.
Identifiers: LCCN 2018050540 (print) | LCCN 2018056561 (ebook) |
  ISBN 9781427121790 (Electronic) |
  ISBN 9780778752226 (hardcover : alk. paper) |
  ISBN 9780778752356 (pbk. : alk. paper)
Subjects: LCSH: Mixed media (Art)--Technique--Juvenile literature. |
  Artists--Biography--Juvenile literature.
Classification: LCC N7433 (ebook) | LCC N7433 .E95 2019 (print) |
  DDC 702.81--dc23
LC record available at https://lccn.loc.gov/2018050540

Crabtree Publishing Company

www.crabtreebooks.com   1-800-387-7650   Printed in the U.S.A./012019/CG20181123

Copyright © **2019 CRABTREE PUBLISHING COMPANY**. All rights reserved. No part of this publication may be reproduced, stored in a retrieval system or be transmitted in any form or by any means, electronic, mechanical, photocopying, recording, or otherwise, without the prior written permission of Crabtree Publishing Company. In Canada: We acknowledge the financial support of the Government of Canada through the Canada Book Fund for our publishing activities.

**Published in Canada
Crabtree Publishing**
616 Welland Ave.
St. Catharines, Ontario
L2M 5V6

**Published in the United States
Crabtree Publishing**
PMB 59051
350 Fifth Avenue, 59th Floor
New York, New York 10118

**Published in the United Kingdom
Crabtree Publishing**
Maritime House
Basin Road North, Hove
BN41 1WR

**Published in Australia
Crabtree Publishing**
Unit 3 – 5 Currumbin Court
Capalaba
QLD 4157

CONTENTS

GET INTO MIXED MEDIA

Read this book with a sense of adventure! It is designed to help you discover and unleash the creativity that exists within you—a creativity that exists within all of us. You will find the projects in this book will help you express your feelings, your thoughts, and your ideas through your art. Create images of your own thoughts and messages you want to share. When learning to create mixed media, enjoy the process and don't worry too much about the finished product. Find your own individual style and run with it!

MINI-BIOGRAPHIES

Throughout the book you will find mini-biographies highlighting the works of well-known artists. You can learn a lot about mixed media techniques by looking at great works of art. Experiment with the techniques the artists used. Examine each artwork to see how its parts were put together, and how **symmetry**, types of lines, and color were used.

WHAT IS MIXED MEDIA?

Artworks are called mixed media when they combine two or more media, or materials. For example, using ink and colored pencils in one work is mixed media. If a work includes beads, photos, fabric, or any other object, that's mixed media, too.

Mixed media became very popular in the 1900s. Before that, artists used mixed media to highlight parts of an artwork. For example, **gold leaf** was often added to make something in a picture, such as a halo, shine. In the early 1900s, artists began questioning the "rules" about art, including whether media should be combined. Famous Spanish artist Pablo Picasso created his first mixed media work in 1912. Today artists mix techniques and materials—and so should you!

Paul Klee (Swiss/German, 1879–1940) used watercolors and printing ink to create *Birds Swooping Down and Arrows* in 1919.

DESIGN ELEMENTS WHEN CREATING MIXED MEDIA

What makes a mixed media artwork interesting? It will depend on the creative use of the elements of design: line, shape, texture, and composition.

Line is the edge between two colors or shapes. It does not have to be straight! Lines can go in any direction and come in any shape, length, or thickness. Artists use lines to draw the viewer's eye in the direction they want it to go.

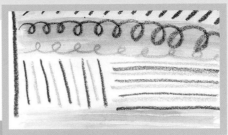

Shape is any enclosed space in a painting. A shape's edges may be created by lines, textures, or colors.

Texture is created in two different ways. Physical texture describes the surface of the artwork, such as smooth or rough. Optical, or visual, texture is the way an artist creates the look of a texture.

Composition is the arrangement of all the shapes, lines, colors, spaces, and textures in a drawing. Artists carefully use these elements so viewers' eyes will follow a path leading to the key, or most important, element or message of the work.

CARL BEAM

(1943-2005) Canada

Ojibwa artist Carl Beam was the first contemporary artist of First Nations heritage to have his work purchased by the National Gallery of Canada. Beam's art explored the tension between **Indigenous** and European settler cultures. In his mixed media works, he kept artistic elements separated to represent the differing views and experiences of the two cultures. Beam used sketches, watercolors, etchings, photos, ceramics, and sculpture in all kinds of combinations. He also added words or objects to reflect both cultures.

Self Validation, Columbia Icefields is an undated work by Carl Beam.

MATERIALS AND COLORS

You can make many of the mixed media art projects in this book with recycled materials found around the house. Collect scraps of fabric and paper, newspapers, poster tubes, magazines, stickers, and toilet-paper and paper-towel rolls. You might also want to use things such as buttons, clay, yarn, beads, and string. You can also use different kinds of art supplies, such as paint, pencils, markers, clay, crayons, pastels, charcoal, ink, glue, and scissors!

Colored pencils can be blended and layered together.

Pastels come in two kinds: oil and chalk.

Old magazines

Brushes come in many shapes and sizes.

Markers

Mixed media art can be made with watercolor paint, acrylic paint, and tempera paint.

WHAT SURFACE TO CREATE ON?

You can use a variety of different materials for the background of your mixed media art. Start with any of these examples: canvas paper, canvas boards, stretched canvas, watercolor paper, fabric, or cardboard. In this book, when the background in a project is listed as art board, any surface can be used. Experiment with different backgrounds. When using watercolor paints, though, it is best to work on watercolor paper. It is absorbent and the paint sinks into the paper. If you use watercolor on other surfaces the paint will just stay on top of the surface. If you use thin paper it will wrinkle and buckle. Make sure your surface will support your creation.

Canvas boards are inexpensive and come in many sizes. They are good for use with acrylic and tempera paints.

Smooth   Rough

Watercolor paper can be smooth or rough. It comes in pads of different sizes and weights.

A palette is a surface to mix paints on. You can buy a plastic one or disposable palette sheets or use a piece of parchment paper.

USING COLOR WHEN CREATING ART

Artists use the color wheel as a tool to help them mix colors. A simple color wheel is divided into two types of colors: primary and secondary. The **primary colors** are red, blue, and yellow. They are called primary because they are the only three colors that can't be made from others. **Secondary colors** are made by mixing two primary colors together.

COMPLEMENTARY COLORS

When choosing colors for your work, keep in mind that colors from opposite sides of the wheel **complement**, or balance, each other. For example, red and green, yellow and violet, and blue and orange are complementary pairs.

WARM AND COOL COLORS

The color wheel also can be divided into warm and cool colors. Color sets the atmosphere, or mood, in a painting. It describes emotions best. Warm colors, such as red, yellow, and orange, are bright and come forward to meet our eye. If you want something to stand out, use warm colors. Cool colors, such as blue, violet, and green, are more calming. They can also appear to **recede**. Using both creates depth in a painting.

TINTS AND SHADES

Tints and shades are variations of a color. Using different tints and shades creates visual interest. A tint is created by mixing white paint with a color. The amount of white added determines how light the tint is. With watercolor paint, you would add water to make different tints. A shade is created by adding black paint to a color. The more black paint that is added the darker the shade. If you add both black and white paint to a color, you create a **neutral color,** such as beige.

Make a color wheel with different media. Draw a circle and divide it into 6 equal pie shapes. Fill in all six colors using a different media for each. Use acrylic paint, watercolor paint, marker, colored pencil, oil pastel, and chalk pastel.

Draw a serpent shape with six sections. Fill the sections using warm colors at the front and cool colors at the back. Notice how the cool colors grow smaller and look as if they are off in the distance.

Tint   *Color + white*

Shade   *Color + black*

Tip

Save all your used acrylic palettes for a fun project at the end of the book.

7

EMOTIONAL PORTRAIT

Create a portrait of a person that illustrates a mood. Think about different moods and ways you can illustrate those feelings. Colors can represent moods. Happiness, sadness, joy, and anger all have colors associated with them. Colors can also have more than one meaning. Cool colors, such as blue and violet, suggest calm and peace, but also sadness. Reds and oranges can be warm and friendly, but also angry and fiery. Artists add to the emotion by using **symbols**. These are images or words that make us feel or remember something unseen.

You Will Need:

- Pencil
- Watercolor paper
- Watercolor paint
- Brushes
- 2 glasses of different sizes
- Oil pastels

PROJECT GUIDES

1 Look at some photos of people looking happy, or look in a mirror and make different happy expressions. Choose one to use in your art.

2 Make a rough pencil sketch of the happy person on your paper. Leave enough room to paint a background.

3 Paint a background with watercolor paint. Wet the paper first and then paint with one color using a very wet brush. Add another color and let them mix together.

4 Color the person using watercolor. Paint on dry paper for the figure. Let it dry.

5 Use symbols to help illustrate the emotion. In this example, colorful bubbles are used to illustrate happiness. Find two glasses that are different sizes. Use a pencil to trace around the glasses. Move the glasses around and trace more circles.

6 Color the circles with oil pastels. Use bright, happy colors. Paint with watercolor to fill in around the pastel and create a bubbly effect.

Try This!

Chameleons are lizards that can change color. Some are black in the morning to absorb heat and white later in the day to reflect it. Many change color for camouflage. Draw a lizard outline and make some copies. Then color them to show different times in a lizard's day!

4

5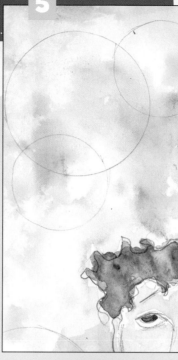

6

(1863-1944) Norway

Edvard Munch used tempera, crayon, and oils to create *The Scream*, which has become a universal symbol of pain and sadness. Munch suffered greatly in his own life. To capture these feelings in his work, he used simple forms and heavy outlines. The figure's strange head looks like a skull. The blue water swirls dangerously, and bands of fiery orange create a threatening sky.

Edvard Munch painted *The Scream* in 1893.

Try This!

Try the exercise again, but illustrate anger this time. What colors represent anger? What kind of symbols could add to the emotion? How do a person's mouth and eyes look when they are angry? Compare your two paintings.

COLORS IN ABSTRACT

Abstract art is art that does not try to represent a figure or environment in a realistic way. Abstract art uses shapes, colors, and lines to communicate its meaning. For example, an artist can illustrate the principles of rhythm, balance, and movement by combining straight lines and geometric shapes. Try this out by cutting shapes from a painted piece of paper and adding them to lines drawn on a paper.

You Will Need:

- Watercolor paper
- Watercolor paint
- Tempera paint
- Brushes
- Markers
- Scissors and ruler
- Glue

PROJECT GUIDES

1 Use a wet brush to cover a piece of watercolor paper with water. Add watercolor paint to your brush and paint. Try to get a variety of tones. Let it dry.

2 On another sheet of watercolor paper, use tempera paint to cover the sheet with many colors. Leave to dry.

3 Cut the sheet of many colors into geometric shapes: circles, rectangles, triangles, and squares.

4 Draw some lines onto the first paper using a fine-tip marker and a ruler.

5 Arrange the shapes on top of the watercolor paper. Play with the design until you have something pleasing. Overlap some shapes.

6 Would it benefit from any more lines? Add them. Glue the geometric shapes to the watercolor paper.

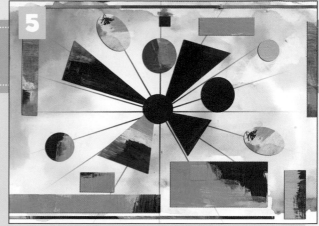

6

JULIE MEHRETU

(1970) Ethiopia/United States

Julie Mehretu aims to capture the spirit of cities and civilizations with her mixed media art. She creates layers of acrylic paint on canvas, and draws on it with pencil, pen, ink, and more paint. She adds cars, buildings, maps, and other city elements, as well as lines to create the feeling of movement and energy.

Mehretu painted *Empirical Construction, Istanbul* in 2003.

SCRATCH ART

This exercise uses a technique called **sgraffito**, or scratching, to create art in a seemingly magical way by revealing hidden colors. Using this technique, paper or poster board is covered with oil pastel, and a coat of paint is painted over top. Scratching away the paint in a design reveals the colors and textures underneath. You can do simple drawings with this technique or more advanced drawings using **hatching** or other marks to fill in large parts of the image. You might try decorating part of a wall in your room—with permission, of course!

You Will Need:

- Canvas paper (2) or poster board
- Oil pastels
- Tempera paint
- Dish soap
- Cup
- Brushes
- Toothpick or skewer

PROJECT GUIDES

1. Start with two pieces of canvas paper or poster board. One will be for practicing making marks and one will be for drawing a picture once you are comfortable with your mark making. Using oil pastels, color designs on the two pieces of paper. It can be an abstract design or blocks of color. Completely cover both pieces of paper.

2. Mix some black and blue tempera paint together in a cup. Add a drop of dish soap. Paint over both oil pastel designs with the paint mixture.

3. Scratch into the wet paint to reveal the colors underneath. You can use a variety of tools such as a toothpick, the end of a paintbrush handle, or a wooden skewer. Test them all to find out which one works best. Try different styles of lines, such as curves, spirals, zigzags, or hatching. Be careful not to rest your hand in the wet paint.

4. On the second piece of canvas paper, draw a picture with the scratching tool of your choice. Draw the outline first.

5. Scratch out the inside of the outlines. Scratch out a border.

Try This!

Repeat the steps but let the paint dry before scratching this time. How is it different? Try drawing a more specific design with the pastels. For example, use greens at the bottom for grass and blues at the top for sky. You can also color a border in all one color. Then scratch your picture out.

3

4

5

HEYWOOD SUMNER

(1853–1940) England

Imagine having not just an art board to work on, but a whole building! Sgraffito has been used for decorating for centuries. It became very popular from about 1890 to 1915. Heywood Sumner used sgraffito to decorate eleven churches and several homes. His designs were scratched and carved out over colored wall plaster.

Heywood Sumner created this sgraffito art of St. Mary the Virgin at a church in Wales, UK.

SPEAKING WITH FABRIC

You Will Need:
- Art board
- Acrylic paint
- Brushes
- Bubble wrap
- Paper towel
- Cloth scraps
- Chalk
- Glue
- Marker
- Scissors

Artists can create meaning visually using symbols and, of course, using letters to form words. Words offer clues to the meaning of the work. Try this exercise that mixes pattern-making with fabric **collage**. Patterns can be made with everyday items found in the home. By pressing the item into wet paint, an image of the item's texture remains when the item is removed.

PROJECT GUIDES

1 Paint your art board with a dark color to provide contrast with the fabric. You can add a small amount of a second lighter color. Apply the paint so that some of the second color is visible, and some is mixed into the wet paint. This creates interesting **highlights**.

2 Make patterns in the paint. Lay a paper towel and bubble wrap on top of the wet paint. Lightly rub your hand over each item. Slowly lift each one up to reveal the pattern left in the paint. Repeat to make more patterns.

3 Gather fabric scraps. (You could cut up old clothes, if you don't have fabric scraps.) Cut the scraps into small pieces. Place in color matching piles.

4 When the paint is dry, trace each of your hands on the art board with chalk.

5 Brush glue inside each hand outline. Place small pieces of fabric on the glue, continuing until both hands are filled in. Add more glue if needed. Wipe the chalk away.

6 Write a message on a piece of fabric with marker. Cut the letters out.

7 Brush glue on the back of each fabric letter. Glue each letter to the art board.

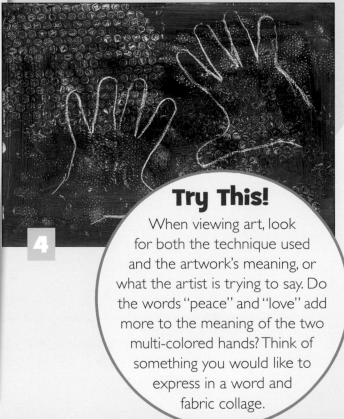

Try This!

When viewing art, look for both the technique used and the artwork's meaning, or what the artist is trying to say. Do the words "peace" and "love" add more to the meaning of the two multi-colored hands? Think of something you would like to express in a word and fabric collage.

JUDY CHICAGO

(1939) United States

Judy Chicago uses her art to deliver political messages, especially about women's rights. Her work often makes use of traditional women's crafts, such as needlework and embroidery, to show that they are just as much art as painting or sculpture. *We're All in the Same Boat* is from a series based on common sayings. Chicago used acrylics, oils, embroidery, and other fabric crafts to create it.

We're All in the Same Boat, 2000.

15

IMAGE TRANSFER

You Will Need:
- Art board
- Acrylic paint
- Brush
- Photocopy of photo or public domain art
- Acryclic gel or Mod Podge
- Sponge
- Stencil
- Scrap paper

Paper image transfer is a way to **imprint** an image from one source onto an art board. Transfers often look ghost-like and add a dreamy look to the artwork you are creating. Plan out your design before beginning. The Rule of Odds is a good rule for composition. This rule states that using an odd number of items for your piece looks more pleasing than using an even number. It creates an interesting composition.

PROJECT GUIDES

1. Paint an art board with a light colored paint. Let it dry.

2. Print or photocopy a **public domain** or clip art image. Something very dark or in **silhouette** works best. Cut the image out leaving a small border.

3. Apply a layer of acrylic gel or Mod Podge to the painted art board. Place the photocopy face down on the board and smooth out all the air bubbles. Wipe away the extra gel. Let it dry.

4. Wet a sponge with water and use it to soak the cutout. Then rub away the paper with your fingers. The image will have transferred to the art board. (Tip: Make sure you rub gently so you don't also remove the transferred image from the board.)

5. Use stencils to add shapes, such as stars or dragonflies, to add visual interest to your art. You can use paint or a marker with the stencil. If using paint, put only a bit on your brush. Using too much paint may cause it to run underneath the stencil. Practice on paper first. Add a word with a letter stencil.

6. Paint a border around the side edges.

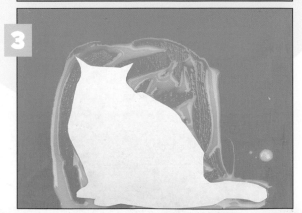

4

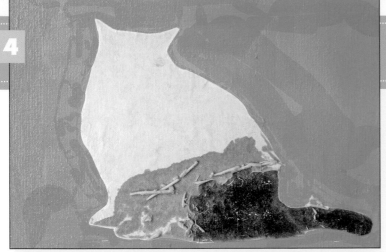

Try This!

Repeat the exercise but this time try using a light colored photo or image. Use stencils and markers to create an interesting background. Sometimes you can see right through the image after the transfer. Experiment with different images to see what different effects you can create.

5

Tip

You can buy stencils or make your own by cutting out a shape or punching holes out of a piece of cardboard. You can use markers or paint with a stencil. Wipe the stencil after each use so you don't transfer paint onto the next place it is used.

6

17

PHOTO INSPIRATION

Many people use quotations as motivation to improve themselves and appreciate life. This project will show you how to create your own **inspirational** mixed media poster using a photo of yourself and a technique called watercolor resist. A resist is a material, such as crayon or glue, that is used by an artist to protect areas in a work from absorbing the watercolor. Take a photo of yourself against a white background, leaving room at the top for your message. Wear an expression on your face that will go with your message.

You Will Need:

- Photo of yourself
- Pencil
- Watercolor paint
- Glue
  (that dries clear)
- Colored pencils
- Marker

PROJECT GUIDES

1. Print your photo in black and white or make a photocopy of it. Paint parts of your shirt and face using a combination of watercolor and colored pencils.

2. Paint the background using a light color of watercolor paint.

3. Write your message across the top using a small squeeze bottle of glue. Let it dry.

4. Paint the background again with a dark color of watercolor paint. Notice how the paint rolls off the glue. This is called watercolor resist.

5. Take a wet brush and lightly brush any drops of watercolor paint off the glue letters.

6. Make a border by rubbing the edge of a marker along the edge of the paper. Outline the letters with the marker to make them stand out more.

4

5

6

Try This!

On a computer or tablet, import your photo into an art app with filters. Try **posterizing** the image. Add type to the image. Experiment until you have totally transformed the original photo.

Did You Know?

Inspiration is what makes people want to create or achieve. The word comes from the Latin *inspirare*, which means "to breathe in." Being inspired is like breathing in an idea.

Just as artists can be inspired to create great art, great art can inspire us to do our best and be better people. Scientists have found that inspirational art really does have a positive effect. What inspires you? Keep a journal of ideas and you'll never run out of inspiration.

LAYERED ART

Mixed media art often involves building up layers of paint. This art style gives you creative freedom. You don't have to use a brush, you can use rollers. Mix paints on the art board by rolling new colors through already painted colors. This exercise involves creating a background, drawing an image, and adding words.

You Will Need:

- Palette
- Acrylic paint
- Small paint roller
- Art board
- Plastic cup
- Cardboard
- Paper
- Marker
- Oil pastel

PROJECT GUIDES

1. Squeeze some paint onto a palette. Roll the paint roller into the paint until the roller is covered. Roll the roller on the art board.

2. Cover a good part of the art board with paint. Alternate using heavy and light pressure on the roller to create texture.

3. Squeeze a different color of paint onto the palette. Roll the same paint roller into the paint until the roller is covered. Roll the roller on the art board. Cover parts of the paint that you rolled onto your art board in Step 2.

4. Repeat Step 3 using other colors of paint until the whole art board is covered.

5. Mix some paint in a plastic cup with enough water to make the mix very watery. Dab it on one end of the painted art board. Tip the board up and let the paint drip. Tip it a different way and let it drip in a new direction. Drag the edge of a piece of cardboard through the paint to smooth it out.

6. While the art board is drying, draw a dog with a black marker on a piece of paper. Leave some areas in your drawing where the paint will show through.

7. When the board is dry, use the sketch as a guide to draw the dog on the art board using a black marker.

8. Add a word or words to your art. Sketch the word with a marker and fill in the letters with paint. Use an oil pastel to make a light, colored outline next to the black marker lines.

Try This!

Try painting your background using sponges instead of rollers. Cover the background surface with one color first, then use a new sponge to add another color. Add a light color. Keep adding layers of paint until you are happy with your background pattern. What else could you use to create a colorful background?

ART FROM ART

Sometimes when you are creating art, you won't be happy with the way your drawing or painting turned out. Mixed media is the perfect art form for **repurposing** old artworks into new art. Repurposing means to find a new way to use something. Is there a portrait you created that you would rather turn into a new piece of art? Be creative with your new portrait. Try using **juxtaposition** and put different-sized items side by side.

You Will Need:

- Art board
- Newspaper
- Glue
- Tempera paint
- Brushes
- Drawing or painting
- Magazines
- Scissors
- Oil pastels

PROJECT GUIDES

1. Make a background for the work. Tear strips of newspaper. Prepare a watered-down glue by mixing equal parts water and glue. Brush the glue on the art board. Lay the strips on the art board, overlapping them until the board is covered. Leave a small border. Let it dry.

2. Lightly brush tempera paint over the newspapers. Make sure you can still see some newspaper through the paint.

3. Take the portrait you are going to reuse and cut out the head part with scissors.

4. Look through old magazines for interesting colors and textures. Look for eyes, hands, and feet. Look for words or sayings. Cut or tear out the pieces.

5. Arrange your magazine pieces to make a body and accessories. Cut or tear them further into the shapes you need. When you are happy with your composition, glue the head and pieces to the background.

6. Make a border around the art board with oil pastels. Add some color to the background.

22

4

5

6

Try This!

On a computer or tablet, import a photo into a photo editing app. Open another image. Copy elements of the second image into the first image to create interesting juxtapositions. Cut and paste different parts of the image. Make some smaller than the original and some bigger.

JUNK TO ART

When is junk just junk and when is junk art? Junk becomes art when the artist who creates the work follows the elements of design—composition, color, lines, and form. **Assemblage** art is created by putting together found objects. Great thought is put into how to arrange the found objects.

You Will Need:

- Art board
- Collection of found objects, such as wire, buttons, old keys, pieces of rope, etc.
- Acrylic or tempera paint
- Paper towel
- Brushes
- Glue or glue gun

PROJECT GUIDES

1 Look for objects to use in your assemblage art. A junk drawer is a great place to start. A thrift store is another place to find objects. Look around and see what you can find.

2 Select a color for the background. Paint the art board. Smudge the paint using a scrunched-up paper towel. Let it dry.

3 Play with the positions of your objects to make a composition. Have one large object as a **focal point** to draw the viewer's eye. Arrange other objects around it in a way that directs the viewer's eye from top to bottom.

4 Paint some of the objects. Let them dry.

5 Start gluing the objects to the art board.

6 Continue gluing the objects to the board and to each other until your composition is complete.

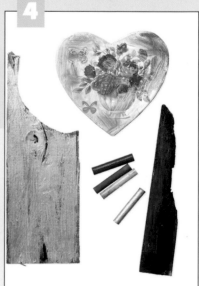

5

6

(1887–1948) Germany

After WWI, much of Germany lay in ruins. Kurt Schwitters decided to collect junk from the streets and turn it into art. He painted found objects and nailed or glued them to a painted board. His careful compositions gave order to the disorder and looked to the future by making something new. He even made up a new word, **Merz**, to describe this kind of art.

Schwitter's *Merz Construction* was created in 1921.

Try This!

Try making an assemblage piece of art out of used packaging: wrappers from candy, pop cans, labels from cans, or any kind of garbage other than food waste. Create a piece of art that demonstrates how packaging materials create waste, which has a negative effect on the environment.

SAY IT WITH TEXTURE

Create an assemblage piece of art that uses symbols to convey a meaning. In this exercise, use the materials to create texture that acts as part of your composition. Use other materials to create the main pieces of your composition. Make use of a **monochromatic**, or single color, scheme to tie all the elements together.

You Will Need:

- Art board
- Tissue paper
- Cheesecloth
- Produce netting
- Gauzy fabric
- Glue
- Acrylic paint
- Brushes
- Twigs, sand, and leaves

PROJECT GUIDES

1 Think of a theme for your assemblage art. In the example shown on these pages, the theme is reaching toward the light and moving away from darkness.

2 Gather the materials for the assemblage. Think of materials that you can use to create texture, such as tissue paper, cheesecloth, produce netting, etc. Also gather materials that can be used as symbols in the work.

3 Cover the art board with glue. Lay the texture materials on top and press them into the glue. This project uses cheesecloth, tissue paper, netting, and gauze. Let it dry.

4 Choose a single color to use for your art. Start with pure, untinted color. Paint on top of the texture across the bottom. Next mix some white paint in it to make a tint of that color. Paint the middle area. Add more white paint for a lighter tint and paint the top area.

5 Glue the symbolic elements to the art board. In this example, twigs and sand represent obstacles and leaves are a symbol of hope.

6 Paint over the new elements.

7 Create a figure from tissue paper. Play with the shape by twisting paper and tearing it.

8 Mix equal parts of water and glue in a cup. Add a blob of paint and stir. Lay the figure on top of the art board. Use a brush to carefully paint the glue mixture on top of the figure. Let it dry.

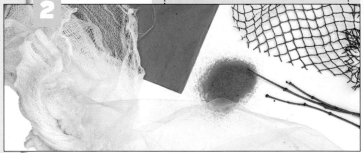

Try This!

This exercise was done with a monochromatic color theme. Next, try making an assemblage of textures using many colors. Does using more colors make it easier to communicate your message?

5

6

7

8

THORNTON DIAL

(1928–2016) United States

Thornton Dial, an African American artist, created assemblages dealing with a wide range of themes, including racism and personal relationships. "I start on a picture when I get a whole lot of stuff together," he explained. "And then I look at the piece and think about life." He created his largest works using spray paint and found objects, such as metal, barbed wire, tree branches, rags, rope, and even bones.

The Man Rode Past His Barn to Another New Day, 1994-1995

PAINT MOSAIC

Now is the time to dig out the used acrylic paint palettes you saved. A used palette of mixed paints can be almost as beautiful as the art itself. It seems a shame to throw it out. If you carefully peel the paint from the palette in one sheet, you will have what is called a paint skin. You can then cut or tear the paint skin. In this exercise, you will create a **mosaic** effect using small pieces of paint skins.

You Will Need:

- Palette covered with dried paint
- Square of fabric
- Pencil
- Glue
- Beads
- Glitter glue
- Scissors (optional)
- Parchment paper
- Brushes

PROJECT GUIDES

1. Take the palette you have saved from previous exercises. Starting at one corner, carefully start to pull the paint off the palette. It should come off in one piece, but it's okay if it tears. Just pull the leftover pieces off as well.

2. Tear the skin into small pieces. If you want the pieces to have smooth edges use scissors to cut the pieces.

3. Draw a butterfly on your piece of fabric. Draw it off-center to make a more interesting composition.

4. Brush glue inside the butterfly sketch. Place pieces of skin on the glue and press down. Continue adding more pieces until the butterfly is filled in.

5. Brush glue over the antenna and glue beads to the fabric.

6. Draw an outline around the butterfly to make it stand out. Make a border using glitter glue or markers.

Try This!

Create a skin without using a dried palette. You can **marbleize** paint by first spreading a light color all over a palette or a piece of parchment paper. Next, drop other colors on top and swirl them with the end of a brush handle or a popsicle stick. Let it dry.

3

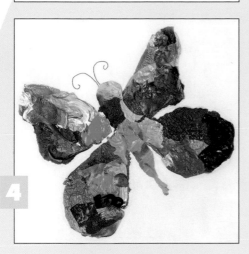

People started making mosaics using small colored stones or pieces of glass thousands of years ago. The ancient Romans decorated homes and public spaces with elaborate mosaics that were so well made they still exist today. In medieval times, people in Italy continued to decorate churches with mosaics. Today, mosaics are popular both as an art form and a craft people can do at home. Mosaics are often seen in large public spaces such as airports. Many more materials are used, including tile, wood, shells, and beads.

4

Roman mosaic of the hero Ulysses, from the second century, now in the Bardo Museum, Tunisia

5

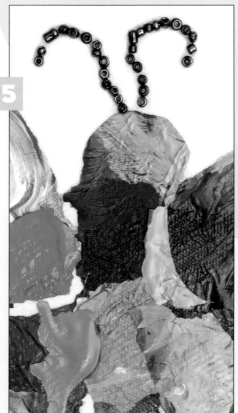

6

29

LEARNING MORE

Books

Art Lab for Kids,
by Susan Schwake, Quarry Books, 2012.

ARTrageous!
by Jennifer McCully, Walter Foster
Publishing, 2015.

The Arts: A Visual Encyclopedia,
by DK, DK Children, 2017.

*Photo Craft: Creative Mixed Media and Digital
Approaches to Transforming Your Photographs*,
by Susan Tuttle, North Light Books, 2012.

Websites

National Gallery of Art
**https://www.nga.gov/education/kids.
html**
NGAkids Art Zone includes descriptions of
interactive art-making tools that are free
to download. You can also explore the
collection of the National Gallery.

Reusable Art
http://www.reusableart.com/
Reusable Art has a collection of copyright-
free and public domain images including
vintage drawings, paintings, and
illustrations.

Tate—A network of four art museums in
the UK
https://www.tate.org.uk/kids
This website features a wonderful
collection of quizzes, art activities to
download, and videos.

Pics4Learning
http://www.pics4learning.com/
This website features a great collection of
photos that students can use for
classroom projects. The images are
copyright-friendly. Includes a great
selection of animal photos.

GLOSSARY

assemblage Three-dimensional art in which found objects are put together in a unique way

collage Artwork that has small items glued to the surface of the paper, canvas, or wood

complement To complete or make better by providing something additional

focal point The area of an artwork that attracts the most attention and draws the viewer's eye

gold leaf A thin sheet of gold used for decorating surfaces

hatching Creating tone or shading by making closely spaced marks

highlights Brighter spots or areas

imprint To make a mark by pressing down

Indigenous Originating from, and belonging to, an area or place

inspirational Giving a person enthusiasm or ideas

juxtaposition Placing elements close together, often for contrast

marbleize To make a surface look like marble

Merz A word invented by artist Kurt Schwitters to describe his assemblage and collage works

monochromatic Having only a single color

mosaic An artwork made from small objects, such as pieces of glass

neutral color A color, such as gray, that is produced by mixing complementary colors; also called earth tones

posterize Print or display a photo or image using a small number of tones

primary colors Red, yellow, and blue, which are the colors from which any other color can be made

public domain A phrase to describe creative works that are not under copyright and can be used by anyone at no cost

recede To grow smaller or weaker, or to move back from something

repurposing Giving a new purpose or use to something

secondary colors Colors that result from mixing two primary colors

sgraffito An art form that requires scratching through a surface to reveal color underneath

silhouette An image showing a face or object as a dark shape on a light background

symbols Words or images that give the feeling of an unseen object or idea

symmetry The qualities of balance, repetition, and harmony in an artwork

INDEX

ABOUT THE AUTHOR

Sandee Ewasiuk is a graduate of OCAD. She has participated in many group and solo exhibitions and her paintings can be found in corporate and private collections around the world. She currently divides her time between painting and teaching art at the Dundas Valley School of Art, The Art Gallery of Burlington, and Fleming College/Halliburton School of Art. She recently spent a month in Thailand as an artist-in-residence, exploring painting and mixed media. Sandee continues to experiment with and explore new ideas and techniques.